PEOPLE OF THE U.S. ARMED FORCES

MARINES

OF THE U.S. MARINE CORPS

by Jennifer Reed

Consulting Editor: Gail Saunders-Smith, PhD

Capstone
press®

Mankato, Minnesota

Pebble Plus is published by Capstone Press,
151 Good Counsel Drive, P.O. Box 669, Mankato, Minnesota 56002.
www.capstonepress.com

1 2 3 4 5 6 14 13 12 11 10 09

Library of Congress Cataloging-in-Publication Data
Reed, Jennifer, 1967 –
    Marines of the U.S. Marine Corps / by Jennifer Reed.
    p. cm. — (Pebble plus. People of the U.S. Armed Forces)
    Includes bibliographical references and index.
    Summary: "A brief introduction to a Marine's life in the Marine Corps, including training, jobs, and life after
service" — Provided by publisher.
    ISBN-13: 978-1-4296-2252-3 (hbk.)
    ISBN-10: 1-4296-2252-0 (hbk.)
    1. United States. Marine Corps — Juvenile literature. I. Title. II. Series.
VE23.R438 2009
359.9'60973 — dc22
                          2008033180

Editorial Credits
Gillia Olson, editor; Renée T. Doyle, designer; Jo Miller, photo researcher

Photo Credits
AP Images/Gerry Broome, 15
Capstone Press/Karon Dubke, 21
Defense Imagery, 5; LCPL Matthew J. Anderson, USMC, 19; LCPL Nicholas J. Galvin, 7
Shutterstock/Drue T. Overby, 1; yossi, 22–23
USAF photo by SSGT Reynaldo Ramon, 17
U.S. Marine Corps photo by Cpl. Andrew J. Carlson, cover; by Cpl. Sheila M. Brooks, 9; by LCPL Marcus D Henry, 11
U.S. Navy Photo by PH3 Julianne F. Metzger, 13

Artistic Effects
iStockphoto/philpell (compass), 2–3, 24
Shutterstock/iNNOCENt (white sand), cover, 1

Note to Parents and Teachers

The People of the U.S. Armed Forces series supports national science standards related to
science, technology, and society. This book describes and illustrates Marines of the U.S. Marine
Corps. The images support early readers in understanding the text. The repetition of words and
phrases helps early readers learn new words. This book also introduces early readers to
subject-specific vocabulary words, which are defined in the Glossary section. Early readers
may need assistance to read some words and to use the Table of Contents, Glossary, Read
More, Internet Sites, and Index sections of the book.

Table of Contents

Joining the Marines

Men and women join

the Marine Corps

to protect the United States.

They work on land,

at sea, and in the air.

Recruits exercise and study

at basic training for 12 weeks.

The Marine Corps has

the longest basic training

in the U.S. military.

Job Training

After basic training,

recruits become Marines.

Next, they train for their jobs.

Some Marines fly helicopters,

like the CH-53E Super Stallion.

Many Marines are infantry.

They are trained

to use weapons

and fight in battles.

Some Marines learn

to drive tanks or AAVs.

AAVs drive on land

and float on water.

13

Living on Base

Marines and their families
live on bases.
Bases are like small towns.
They have stores, hospitals,
and homes.

The Marine Corps

has 21 bases.

Bases are in the United States

and around the world.

Serving the Country

Most Marines serve

for four years.

Career Marines stay

in the Marine Corps

for at least 20 years.

After serving, Marines leave

the Marine Corps.

They are then called civilians.

As civilians, they go to college

or find jobs.

Initial Complaint Report

Control #: av88013
Date reported: 03/19/04
Time reported: 18:24

POLICE
NORTH

21

Glossary

AAV — a vehicle that drives on land and floats on water; AAV stands for Assault Amphibian Vehicle.

base — an area run by the military where people serving in the military live and military supplies are stored

basic training — the first training period for people who join the military; basic training is sometimes called boot camp.

career — relating to the type of work a person does

civilian — a person who is not in the military

infantry — a group of people in the military trained to fight on land

recruit — a person who has just joined the military

Read More

Kaelberer, Angie Peterson. *U.S. Marine Corps Assault Vehicles*. Military Vehicles. Mankato, Minn.: Capstone Press, 2007.

Reed, Jennifer. *The U.S. Marine Corps*. Military Branches. Mankato, Minn.: Capstone Press, 2009.

Internet Sites

FactHound offers a safe, fun way to find educator-approved Internet sites related to this book.

Here's what you do:

1. Visit *www.facthound.com*
2. Choose your grade level.
3. Begin your search.

This book's ID number is 9781429622523.

FactHound will fetch the best sites for you!

Index

Word Count: 168
Grade: 1
Early-Intervention Level: 22

24